Songs from the Depths

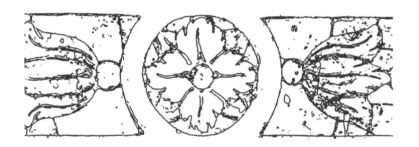

poetry

by

Beth Anne Boardman

978-1-950186-25-9

Cover Painting by Gail Broadbent Firmin
Cover Design by Jennifer Leigh Selig
Interior Art by Beth Anne Boardman

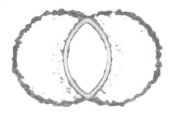

MANDORLA BOOKS
WWW.MANDORLABOOKS.COM

To My Babies

and their babies

∞

To Chris + Linea

with so much
love + so
many thanks for
the wonderful women
+ writers that you
are? ♡ Brett

Table of Contents

∞

Part III: Gloaming

Part IV: Ceremony

Part V: Blessing

Foreword

∞

As I read Beth Boardman's insightful meditative poems in this new volume, I could not help but think of the relation between poetry and prayer. All of the poems she includes carry a prayerful tone and depth. Clearly, prayer, akin to poetry, is a deeply imagined experience that can move us to the edge of mystery and to the ineffable by allowing us a glimpse of a deeper, more fully dimensional view of reality.

Prayer, like poetry, is an act of imagination; the former contains or harbors a form of *poiesis,* a Greek word that suggests a making or forming or shaping something into a coherent form. One cannot help but sense Beth's struggles and achievements as she negotiates that narrow gap between poetry and prayer, if indeed there is a gap at all.

Her volume is also enriched by having a line illustration from her photography for each poem, a perfect blend of word and image. Not a starkness, really, but a deep simplicity hovers around each of the poems, like this from "The Unknown Bell," which after a series of meditations, ends with

> how is it
> that I feel
> the ringing of that bell
> here inside my heart? (p. 26)

Her insight throughout this poem and others is that very little takes place in the phenomenal world that does not have "a cunning duplicate in the mind," as Melville writes in *Moby-Dick.*

In "Amazement is a Choice," Beth brings up one of her favorite themes: remembering:

> I remember hearing my husband's soft voice
> crooning to our little son
> on the patio outside our bedroom window—
> and my son's lilting voice,
> asking the most adorable questions about bugs.... (p. 30)

The last line ending in an ellipsis is part of her poetic signature. An ellipsis is a fascinating poetic device; it suggests an invitation by opening a gap, or designating something unfinished. As readers we are invited to help complete the stanza or the poem; perhaps the poet has more to say, but not just now. I find that the poems breathe through the ellipses that each of her poems contains.

"Forgive Me" is one of several poems in the second person, creating an intimacy with the reader and the subject matter. I like the tension it sets up as well:

> Forgive me if
> grief and joy live side by side
> in this altar, my heart....
>
> Forgive me if I forget
> that mistletoe
> festoons itself over dying branches, (p. 87)

The poem's final images are salvific, soothing and reconciling. They offer the voice that laments and seeks forgiveness through a reconciling alternative:

> This is the place
> where God whispers!
>
> And where I realize
> the answer to all of my problems

is *thank you....* (p. 88)

One of my favorite poems is "Birds and Rain" because the ordinariness of an early image is both familiar to us and arresting:

> I opened the car door
> outside a filled church,
> and in poured this majesty:
>
> a stirring wind,
> a brush of warm water,
> a pure clear note arcing, falling, landing
> from some high, secret place.... (p. 33)

Where does God reside, asks the poem: in the packed church? Outside in "a brush of warm water"? Yes and yes. What moves me in these lines is the presence of mystery in the ordinary, a sensibility that Beth shares with poets like Mary Oliver, Jorie Graham, Walt Whitman, Naomi Shihab Nye and others. Here is one of many illustrations where poetry is so akin to prayer.

"Ribbons and Stardust" is one of the best poems in the collection, as I see it. Here Beth remembers her ancestors through beautiful details, including what she learned from her mother

> In my mothering,
> I sometimes sense my mother....
>
> Sometimes her sadness and despair
> creep across the corners of my eyes—
> but less and less,
> as I uncover her love
> and my love
> and our love.... (p. 9)

Remembering itself is a form of mothering. All of us can reflect on the way we become our parents in small but crucial ways that define our own identity in the shadows of our ancestors. What I like in this and other poems is Beth's unadorned honesty about the place of sadness and despair in our lives; but always what redeems, not deletes these emotions, is love itself as a healing attitude which cultivates a sense of self-forgiveness for our imperfections.

"Wandering Courage" takes us deeper into the mystery of being imperfect and prevailing in the face of it.

> I wonder if
> the willingness to stand
> in the chill wind of
> the vast unknown—
> if that is not courageous, too....
>
> •
>
> I feel a kinship
> with all things crushable: (p. 60)

The last two lines are among the most powerful in the collection. Not "crushed" or "crushing" but "crushable," the ability to be crushed, even, perhaps, the willingness to be crushed. And then to this last observation the poem entertains:

> Maybe waking up
> to the mysterious generosity of darkness
> is where Courage lives.... (p. 61)

What begins to form as I read through the entire collection is a world-view, perhaps a soul-view, seen through the stories each tells, each like a negotiation between two worlds: the one we present to the world and the interior stillness of the soul's ponderings. Beth sustains this tension remarkably throughout the collection.

I end this brief excursion into a handful of her poems with another that I hold great affection for: "Among the Gratitudes." It is the last poem of the volume and reveals where Beth's heart resides: In that quiet space in each of us that is grateful for the gifts, even those that can wound us deeply, because it is necessary to comprehend the deep mystery of being itself.

> Perhaps
> holding a spot
> for Silence within
>
> serves the greater good....
> Amid the cacophony
> of modern life,
>
> the chatter
> of thoughts, (p. 112)

"Perhaps" is one of Beth's favorite operative words: always wondering, not wanting to pin things down too securely, and being available to be surprised. Her poems are continual surprises at life's uncertainties bumping up against life's claimed securities. In the tension between these two is the ellipses of life . . . where we are asked to fill in what we live and how we live it. Her poems are fine and lasting guides to such a meditative place of prayer.

Dennis Patrick Slattery, PhD

Emeritus Faculty of Mythological Studies, Pacifica Graduate Institute and author of *Casting the Shadows: Selected Poems*; *Just Below the Water Line: Selected Poems*; and *Feathered Ladder: Selected Poems with Brian Landis*

Part I

Mystery

Midnight Wind Chimes

Wandering around the house at midnight,
on a secret mission
(for Tums
or Advil
or something else I've forgotten) –

I am akin to Silence:
we are partners in the night.

Creeping through darkness,
we do our care-full duties.

•

Breezes
stir windchimes on the deck,
drawing my gaze outward:

I see Moon's silverglow
muffled under wooly clouds

and beneath, birds hunker....

•

Silence and I pause on our rounds
and take in the breeze,
the chimes,
the hunkering birds,
and we hug ourselves just a little bit –

grateful for shelter,
and children,
and each other....

~~~~~

How Boring to be Human

I am glad that,
as it turns out,

I live a life
bedazzled by mystery.

•

Sometimes
walking the beach,
my imagination swirls out
over diamond-touched
waves....

Sometimes
miniature tangerine roses
outside my front door
seem to give me three tiny smiles
as I walk by—

and I love them so for blooming.

Is this not normal?

•

A vast
web of feelers
anchor love onto the earth
and can't stop themselves doing it....

They are people
kept awake at night
by someone else's suffering,
who, to fend off helplessness,
send out care.

These are the things that make me pray in the black night:
love,
love,
and love....

•

Whatever else
these whispered blessings do—
on the next night that you turn and toss
with your human worries,

know that somewhere
good wishes flow—
even though it's three a.m.,
and most likely the wisher also wishes for sleep....

•

Although sometimes I can't imagine myself
into the next moment,

I am glad—

because somehow
this grief pushes me deeper
into the great mystery that I live.

•

No one knows exactly
what causes a child to be born,

or a seed to sprout forth a tiny rootling—
even science hasn't found those exact
neuro-bio-chemical triggers.

Yet science and I at last
must stop measuring—

only metaphor
can explain the inexplicable....

•

Each moment connects me
to the greatness that is you,
my friend—

to the mystery
that we all lie here at night
completely exposed to the universe....

•

On quiet evenings
I can hear the world
turning underneath its bustle.

Its faint music quivers
through windows thrown open
to warm autumn air....

When it seems
like anguish
may etch itself into my face forever,

I remember the thousand miracles,
and I am glad to be a lover of mystery—

how boring, otherwise,
to miss all of this grandness!

~~~~~

Ribbons and Stardust

They visit me at the oddest times,
my ancestors—

a song, a scent, a waft
of southern breeze upon my cheek—

it takes stillness
to sense them.
So that is something to cultivate.

Maybe in seeking stillness,
we invite them?

I like to think that.

In my mothering,
I sometimes sense my mother....

Sometimes her sadness and despair
creep across the corners of my eyes—
but less and less,
as I uncover her love
and my love
and our love....

How much she taught me
about the preciousness

of life, of love,
of music, of rosy cheeks,
of handmade things,
of baking,
and clean sheets....

How she and my father
made birthdays and holidays
the two special times in a year
when we laid aside strife
and embraced magic....

She told stories
of our ancestors:

how the hills around Bartlett, Texas
crept so far into my granddaddy's heart
that he spent the rest of his life

writing about them—
how music flowed like blood
through my grandmother's being,

and my mother's.

My father told how,
living at the foot of the lake,
his extended family
wove their
wreaths of history—

how woodworking,
land-walking,
dairy farming,
hunting,
popcorn, and
mincemeat
all settled into
our fireside stories.

How I ache that my life
and my children's lives
have rippled away
from a centering story.

Modern life whisks us beyond the
currents of ancestry—
but now as I get older,
I remember them often,
and I want to tell their stories.

Especially on their death days,
I remember parents,
and their parents,
and theirs—

the winding strands of their DNA
loop and twine within me,
within my curious children....

Mulling on ribbons and stardust,
on past and future,
sadnesses, losses,
I bless them all.
I bless their errors, their callousness,
I bless their love and
their best intentions.

Prayers ribbon backward
and forward in time—

they rain like stardust on our children....

~~~~~

Lone

When birds sing,
    (which, if you really listen,
      is most of the time)
I cannot feel lonely.

They do go quiet sometimes—
    (then I wonder
      if they are exhausted
      or hopeless
      or fleeing something.)

Plowing, paving, planting,
changing, filling, draining
obscures their song.

They always sound again though—
proof of Magic, I have decided!

Evidence of the Artist:
Blackbirds over raucous playgrounds,
Hummingbirds, obviously,
Hawks aloft (dodging Blackbirds.)

The Humor of the World
dreamed these
    sound sparkles
    that fall through time
    like glitter,

so that day or night we can know:
Magic lives.
(Rejoice.)

~~~~~

Blossoming
(The Oracle of the Well)

This morning
I awoke to insistent hummingbirds
buzzing outside my window.

No flowers in my garden,
yet here they are!

I noticed sun,
soft air, blue sky.

After a year of Loss,
I decided, on this lovely day,
to go see the Woman at the Well....

I found her sitting,
her head on her knee, curled up in the lee
of a sunlit stucco wall.

She looked up at me and spoke
after a very long time:

> *I'm afraid*
> *I have very little to offer you*
> *at the moment,*

she said.

> *I would like to say something uplifting....*

> *I would like to be articulate*
> *and use sparkling verbs.*

> *I would like to astound you with*
> *insight, wisdom, stunning imagery —*
> *something.*

> *At the moment, though,*
> *words have left me.*

> *They were the last things to go.*

> *This year took everything.*

> *It will all return, on the great*
> *wheel of life.*

> *But for now, my dear,*

15

my well is empty....

She patted the ground next to her,
stirred her skirts out of the way,
said:

> *You are welcome to sit here*
> *with me, though —*
>
> *and experience*
> *the oracle of yourself.*

So I sat down with her,
peaceful, in the sun.

The quiet took hold.

I felt like a lizard, maybe,
or some other life-form that needs
warm radiance to feel alive.

My thoughts drifted back
over this year of death,
heartbreak,
illness....

Vulture medicine in play, I thought.

Perhaps I must sit here until
I pick my own bones clean....

I nodded off

and the visions began....

A cougar appeared at my shoulder,

warm and tawny.
Her pelt smelled of wild grass and sunshine.
I felt woozy and unsure—
she gave the nape of my neck a tiny nudge
with her moist nose

then loped away,
power coiled in her muscles like springs....

Befuddled, I tried to stir—
but lulled by the hum of the bees in the lavender,
I drifted off again.

Through a crack in the night,
I saw a triangle of turquoise sky,
and a huge black raven in
silhouette.
The raven sat in silence,
regal and affectionate.

No words,
no directions,
no messages.

A sudden fresh wind
stirred against my cheek—

my eyes opened to
sweet golden light.
I got up, dewy and shaky,
like a newborn foal or fawn,

like I was fresh from the womb
and not ready for public viewing....

I walked over to the
edge of the mountain and stood,
having no idea whether
I was going up or down,
but enjoying the view,
and the beautiful wind....

Before I left her that day,
I went back
to the woman at the well
to say goodbye.

She looked up at me
with turquoise eyes
and said one last thing:

>   You've given all you had to your blossoming.
>   This emptiness is sacred.

>   It's quiet and the beings are visiting....

>   All is well.

Now,
as the days go by,
I sweep around the empty well
and keep the pail and dipper dusted.

~~~~~

Midnight—

has become
my favorite time of night,

poised between days,
between waning and dawning,
between loss and discovery.

•

Once I knew a woman
with teeth bright as stars,
a smile passionate as a desert sunrise.

She lit up a room,
drew the gazes of passersby.

Her skin, white as old porcelain,
thin and fragile as tissue,

carved and creased with story,
belied a soul
thriving in the between—

even in broad daylight.

•

Sometimes we must give up
the present
and even
the hope of the future.

We stand between time,
see no opposites.

We are old *and* young,
happy *and* sad,
enlivened *and* entombed.

We are Midnight.

•

Stone and light,
ending and beginning:

our own abysmal faults,
our colossal miscalculations
and oversights,
our blatant humanity

demand to be drawn
into the circle of our love.

Kindness:
the gold
within the gold.

~~~~~

Part II

Green

The Unknown Bell

On my way through
the wilderness,

I heard a bell in the distance....

I could not tell
whether it was the single
ringing chime from a church –

or a temple-bell
through the trees.

Silence followed....

Birds fluted
and busied themselves,
hopping from branch to branch
carrying urgent twigs....

Insects chattered
among rustling grasses....

Leaves brushed by one another
in their softly swaying dance....

Continuing, questioning—
feeling touched, nonetheless,
by the great unknown,

again the bell sounded
at the edge of my hearing,

bringing my step
up short,

causing me to pause
like a doe in a clearing,

all senses on high alert....

A swirl of wind,
a falling leaf,
a brilliant sky,

how is it
that I feel
the ringing of that bell
here inside my heart?

~~~~~

A Low Winter Sun

A hawk cries
under
this low winter sun....

(I wonder if hawks pray
for the return of light.)

With a few strong wing-beats
and supreme aerodynamic design,

the great talons let go and
glide out over snowy expanses,
electrifying to witness
(powerful, eternal, unquestioning.)

While we cower or shiver or snuggle-down
and count the days to longer light,
to hope and warmth,

the hawk searches for food,
regular as the sunrise—

surveys the ground,
rides the updrafts,
expends its precious energy
only when necessary.

All its movements efficient
and filled with a grace so stunning that

in the face of our constant
human doubt,
our frantic celebrations
and incantations,

we stand still
and thrill to its call.

This is faith:
outside of our suffering thoughts,
all of nature functions in
flawless rotation—

every day demonstrating
the perfect operation
of mystery....

~~~~~

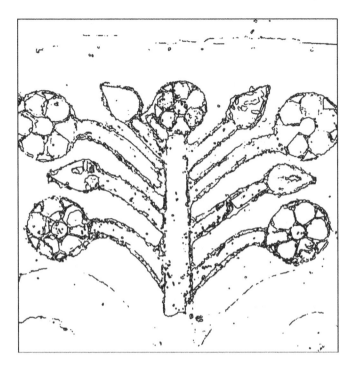

Amazement is a Choice

Amazement is a choice—

green leaves are not.

Here are the things that amaze me:
everything—

but only if I sit still and stop worrying.

Mary Oliver says that there is singing in a leaf—
I believe her.

I'm pretty sure I've heard them singing to me,
or at least whispering....

I remember
hearing great sheaves of palm fronds
murmuring over me
as I napped
in the middle of a sundrenched June,
cradling the jumping daughter inside me.

I remember hearing my husband's soft voice
crooning to our little son
on the patio outside our bedroom window—
and my son's lilting voice,
asking the most adorable questions about bugs....

All these long years of happiness and disaster later,
these memories still bring sweet tears to my eyes,

and those palm fronds still whisper....

I'm convinced
what they whisper
are blessings.

And now I know the secret of amazement:

amid chaos,
noisy bars,
midtown traffic,

if I can just remember to touch it,
Silence flows everywhere....

How else have the Wise Ones
developed such deep laugh lines?

Practicing their buddha smiles,
they've been finding amazement

in the dirt,
in love,
in despair and tragedy,
in rain and mud and starvation and dancing,

in shattered last breaths....

Some call it Magic,
some call it God,
and some miss it altogether,

racing around in their twirling dramas.

And that, my lovely friend,

that is amazing too.....

~~~~~

Birds and Rain

I hear God in birdsong and rain,

when a million green leaves rustle
under a breeze
laden with tiny droplets.

How do their faint notes echo so far
in this loamy rich forest?

I opened the car door
outside a filled church,
and in poured this majesty:

a stirring wind,
a brush of warm water,
a pure clear note arcing, falling, landing
        from some high, secret place....

How could I leave?

World without end....

~~~~~

Hurry

Mockingbirds, heal me
Ravens, heal me
Rain, heal me

Southeasterly breezes
bringing unfamiliar sounds,
Heal me

Sounds of kitchen
Sounds of neighbor
Sounds of every new day,
Heal me

Open windows,
Heal me

Red canyons,
Heal me

Silver trees,
Heal me

Faint green leafy mist,
Heal me

And hurry.

Warmth
Light
Bees,
Heal me.

God is outside

And why I must live
With the windows
Open.

Heal me

And hurry

Thank you.

~~~~~

Feather Rain

Some wounds
would take the whole earth
to heal.

Last night
soft rain danced
like feathers
through my open window.

Slipstreaming
through almost still air,
fine droplets carried their
slight secrets.

Like shivers
through a web,

I felt their whispers
of comfort.

I remembered once hearing
the Great One
speaking to me
through desert boulders.

I had leaned my tired head
against their warmth;
they radiated a whole day's worth
of desert sun
into my fearful heart.

> *Listen:*
> *I have been here since the beginning.*
> *I've seen everything there is to see.*
> *You are no worse*
> *and no better*
> *than anyone—*
> *keep going....*

Some wounds we carry our whole lives,
like amputations.

What was torn out
exists only in the other world—
in ashes,

in dreams.

This soft gentle rain
falls on everyone,
everyone....

I turn my face up to it
and stay very quiet, listening.

I feel Love
seeping right down into
this suffering heart....

Everyone,
everyone
is worthy of this
deep and private love.

~~~~~

40

A Recipe for Plum Salsa

Sipping coffee &
chopping jalapeños:

I'm certain my mother never did
these things of an afternoon!

Still, I feel connected to her—
to all those who mother—
who stand at kitchen sinks
as the sun streams in,
wind blowing through the [plum] trees.

Maybe it's the dust of this land
that's gotten into my essence,
infusing its nature and needs.

We consume the land we live on—
its molecules build themselves
into our bodies.

Shall we listen?
Can we feel it?
Communion.

You can stand at any window,
eat any food,
breathe any air,
and feel
how different you are not.

There is simply no reason
for your soul to be so hungry.

~~~~~

Part III

Gloaming

At the End of the Known

In the last years,
so much leaving;

a time of silence
on incoming clouds.

Some kinds of change
wrest us.

Facing into floods and
whistling winds, words ebb.

Life at the edge of living,
seated at the end of the known: equipoint.

Between coming and going:
a negotiated peace.

Between earth and air,
there is no teacher—

no guides, no hope or blame,
only listening;

no voice
but the quiet one within....

How I've loved
the noise of love,

the chaos of bustle,
busyness, children!

I spoke my dreams
to the Great Listener

and watched them drift
into the evening sky.

Then I heard it:
Love and Silence.

Everyone's secret;
few seek it.

~~~~~

Love and Grief

Can we really
practice Gratitude?

Can we really
dwell in Love?

Loss comes,
dressing us in black,
sending us inwards
and down.

From our knees
we struggle to find them:

Gratitude and Love,
distant balloons, floating into the sky.

Arriving, the Queen of Grief
settles into her underworld throne,
a silent, ardent teacher.

•

Some weeks ago,
at a memorial for a well-beloved,
a stranger turned to me and said:
> *All problems point to where*
> *more love is needed.*

•

Love and Grief:
two faces of one coin.

Neither deity rules alone.

Let their slow rule
hone, humble, bless us.

Break open to either
and your own shards
will deepen and free you.

~~~~~

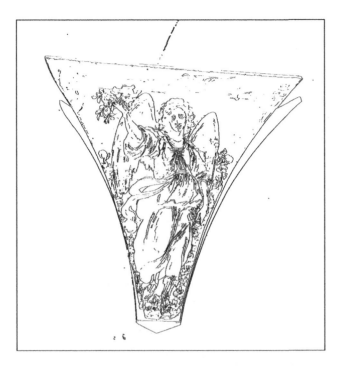

A Surge of Angels

Living feels like a long, hard slog
through darkness sometimes.

If not the actual darkness
of loss, illness, death,
then an imagined darkness.

No respite, no ending, no light
at the end of the tunnel—

our bodies know no difference between
the real and the imagined.

The antidote to wrenching times?
Allow your soul to be wrenched.

Between the shards, our essences well—
ideas, wishes, arguments,
old and new dreams.

Like Buddha under the Bodhi Tree,
in the space of loss and in the quiet of an emptied mind,
we can feel the fabric uniting the universe.

In the stillness of sorrow,
angels surge around our struggling shoulders.

Life waits for us to notice it.

You have the secret!

Your delight in the cacophony of leaves,
in standing naked
under the moonbeams
in your bedroom,
in music floating from a window,
or the smell of bread baking down the street.

Like the Old Ones say,
the only fools
are lonely fools.

~~~~~

The Storykeepers

I am the mouthpiece of my ancestors,
the advocate of the yet unborn.

Once, I felt I was packed away
in dusty boxes
with yellowed labels.

•

After a life
of intense activity,

a certain stillness
haunts.

•

A young funny / crazy woman
and her children used to live here.

She told them stories
late into the nights—

and I used to listen.

•

Old family tales gather
in the between-times,

and among them,
some glowing pearls:

> *magnolia trees*
> *hunting leases*
> *gun oil*
> *boiled coffee and flapjacks*
> *sunny flat rocks*
> *distant pines*
> *tea dances*
> *recitals*
> *drums*
> *feathers*
> *cornbread*
> *rocky canyons*
> *arrowheads on Sunday mornings*
> *candied pecans*
> *and a bowie knife in the door—*

stories of the grandfathers
and the grandmothers.

•

> *Hope grows*
> *in dark places survived.*

•

Our unfolding never stops.
Everything offers us its life!

>   *Wisdom lives*
>   *in fire and stone and night.*

•

This is no time for the living dead!

Someone needs to
keep the stories,
tell them to the children
over candlelight,

weave the magic of history
at the side of a crackling fire.

•

You are the mouthpiece of your ancestors,
you are the advocate for those yet unborn.

~~~~~

Piano

Life whirls,

blows in
through open windows
and doors.

That puff of air against my face
can halt me.

I sense a cadence
within the rush
and routine
of daily living,

a sort of miraculous rhythm
of comings and goings,

haves and haven'ts,

old age and death,

uncomfortable pregnancies,
delirious births,
iridescent joy,
rending grief....

Pausing at the threshold,
I am aware of life's notes

running and chasing and loving
each other across
the keys of a distant piano.

Despite despair,
abreast of beauty,

I stand enwrapped
by eternity.

•

Once,
on the way up into
an indelibly still,
exquisitely soft,
grey, whispery dawn—

up from deep,
peaceful,
midnight blue
dreams,

I heard the river rushing by me again.

It was like waking
to God,
to a lover's touch.

I and the river
and the wind
and the sound—

the air,
the light,
the dark,
the depth—

we lay blended into
one moment.

I couldn't tell whether I was by the river—
or was the river....

When the night-current
finally buoyed me up
to full wakefulness,
the love-song of the river merged

into tires, whooshing
on a distant motorway.

I lay bereaved.

Oh my river!

What incandescent cruelty
to find you turned into
a highway!

•

Yet inside me these things still dwell:

the silence, the river, the dawn,
the darkness, the light....

And now and then,
singularity re-expresses itself

through a puff of breeze
across a sunny expanse,

through sounds of friendly voices
wafting up from sidewalks below,

through a single piano note
wandering through the air—

dropped

like a curtsey,

upon my delighted ear....

~~~~~

Wandering Courage

Is it Courage that makes small
thrushes sing in the grey dawn
after a wildfire—

or Courage that keeps
the last ember glowing,
unaccountably,
after a dousing?

Maybe ocean waves exhibit Courage
when they show up all turquoise and glossy
the day after a storm,

or Great Horned Owl boasts Courage
when it calls out into the black silence
of the night forest.

•

Soldiers tell me they don't feel courageous
as they rush forward into war,
yet they go—
and that must be Courage.

I've cared for children
who, as they receive chemotherapy,
exude streams of Courage
from their very fingertips....

I wonder if
the willingness to stand
in the chill wind of
the vast unknown—
if that is not courageous, too....

•

I feel a kinship
with all things crushable:

tiny spiders under my feet,
small lizards, lying exposed on my front steps,
delicate lavender petals floating down
from the jacaranda trees.

On this planet,
all are tiny,
fragile,
crushable—

but like the diamond stars,
we glow
in pitchest
black.

Maybe waking up
to the mysterious generosity of darkness
is where Courage lives....

~~~~~

Ubique Silentium

I found an old poem written
on a warm day
(I remember an offshore wind whipping foam
backwards off of crashing surf.)

Here's the truth,
          the poem said,
I no longer believe in true love.

Oh! Sad! (I thought.)

[How long ago did I write this? Why?]

I believe in Silence and Space
and the Great Unknown—

the place I have always feared.

Silence: a cold, interstellar
sort of place, at first—
terrifying. Huge.
Endless.
Like standing in the mouth of
a vast black cavern....

•

Healers, yogis, holy people tell us:
    In Silence Lives All Possibility

We humans, though,
will hop like jack-rabbits,
dance like deer
(I've done these things myself)
to outrun Silence.

•

Silence contains
the Grail.

Truth,
Love,
Tristan and Iseult,
Arthur, the Green Knight,
God, Spirit, Mary,
the Prophet,

the Buddha,
the Four Directions—

listen, say these tales:
>   *Accept your existence.*
>   *Make a hospitable place for your dreams.*

One night, I steeled myself
to stand in the chill of the vacuum within me.

I did not disappear!

Instead
I found a dearness in myself.

Surprise!

All my loves have deepened.

~~~~~

Part IV

Ceremony

Juniper Dreaming

Scent of juniper
on the night wind—

velvet elk in the
near shadows—

rolling voices—
distant

jingle of bells,
crack of gourds:

grey dawn
on ceremony day.

•

Juniper on my pillow
at the black

of midnight—
reawakening,

reviving,
retying me

to the past,
the future,

messages crossing
time, distance, rocky bluffs.

•

Recalling
scrub juniper,

rocks and sand
(my companions),

mists and winds
(my mantles.)

•

Never alone,
with a lifetime
of miracles
memories

priests
shamans

poets
goddesses

children
ancestors....

Replete with images,
adventures,

alive,
waiting....

Juniper,
calling....

I,
arriving....

~~~~~

A Waltz of Owls

I am happy the owls own the night—
their quiet announcements shake me.

They are my secret call to order:

to inventory my dreams
and requisition Grace

and remember
that I dance

with golden ghosts.

~~~~~

Web Love

We sat in a circle praying for ourselves—
surrounded by food, warmth, comfort.

None of this diminished
the earnestness of our prayers.

Every golden-hearted woman shone with Love.

All had sailed near Death,
grown despite Trauma.

Tattooed by Earth's grinding,
we stilled our thoughts,
sank into the warm safety of one-another,
and listened:

> *Dear ones,*
> *you have earned this comfort, yes.*
>
> *But remember the Golden Web*
> *that surrounds this Earth –*
> *the one that aided you*
> *in your time of despair.*
>
> *All across the world,*
> *others now need you.*
>
> *I am here to join this*
> *loving circle and remind you:*
>
> *hold the suffering in your hearts*
> *every moment,*
> *just like the Old Ones held you*
> *in theirs. Recall.*

Touch the Web with your thoughts.
Send the others strength
as we sent you strength.

Congratulations and welcome
to the other side of the Web.

In Silence we knew our real work
had just begun.

~~~~~

Day and Night/Silent Wings

Day and night
my house is surrounded
by sacred wings.

Two hawks call to each other across my roof
in the still dawn;

their *scree*s grace the silence.

They rise on currents of air
lifted by the difference between night and day,
cold and warm,
dark and light.

Sometimes the hawks reappear at noon,
side-slipping and floating on updrafts
rising from warming hillsides.

Their calls ring like temple bells,
reminding me to be still for a moment,
to stop and touch the eternal in the day,
to take a breath and offer myself to the Mystery.

One calls
as the sun turns orange
and sinks into
a blanket of clouds
drawn over the western ocean.

This one summons the night-shift:
those who soar in the darkness
as I sleep,
dream,
and sometimes dance.
If you're outside walking
through a warm coastal dusk,
oohing and *ahing* over the glint of
rare blue-diamond stars,

you can sometimes catch a glimpse
of white wings glowing high above,
coming in fast,
and soon gone—
right over your head,
without a sound.

A sheerly distant whistle
drifts somewhere behind
those silent wings,
testimony
to their untouchable presence.

On the very darkest nights,
there is One
who comes to the roof-corner
adjoining my bedroom—

and even though the window might be closed
against the damp and chill,
he announces his landing
with a piercing cry:

I am here for the night.

I sleep and wake
under the jurisdiction
of sacred wings.

~~~~~

This Time, I Listen

Raven calls,
my heart thrills.

This throaty voice
floating across the silence
seems a private note
between us.

•

Memory transports me
to the lip of
an echoing red stone canyon
in the translucent predawn,

to the edge of a Hopi mesa,
pre-ceremony.

Raven's voice seemed to
summon the dancers,
cue the singers
with their rattles and bells.

What glorious magic
has unfolded over the years
whenever I took Raven's hint
to pause, listen.

•

Years ago
Raven called me
to an assignation
with Solitude.

I ran from it.

I was in such a hurry to live....

This time,
I listen.

I know
the curves of your black feathers,
the firmness of your claws.

•

I recall the
power of solitude—

I step into it
as naturally as I step into
a garment;

its velvet swirl
enfolds me.

Oh, I know this step!
It's a compelling, dangerous dance....

•

Trickster Raven!
I hear you cackle when
I sink into the illusion of aloneness!

How can I forget again?

> The graces of the universe
> weave around us....

> Atoms innumerable riot within us....

I,
(who can feel so proficient
in my solitary walk)

I am the center of a circle
of generous beings
clamoring for my notice
night and day—

from the cells living within me,
to the spiders in my garden.

> *The whole breadth*
> *of the spirit world*
> *holds us,*
> *embraces*
> *our every ragged breath.*

•

> *Throw off your cloak of delusion!*

> *Your pockets are filled*
> *with the riches of the universe!*

> *Your very touch teems with beings.*

•

Oh Love,
this time I listen!

~~~~~

Ceremony

One night
I sat, it seemed,
at the bottom of
a great empty bowl....

The flat ground spread
away from me,

the vast, deep
luminous lavender sky
melted backwards into space
above me.

All around me
a great hollowness
rose up to meet infinity.
Birds held their breath,
the breeze settled,

even my thoughts
filed out

to gaze
at that lucent expanse.

Between me and the next star:

nothing!

The quiet deepened,
the sunset darkened.

•

Space unveils itself
before our watching eyes.

Each day we witness
the great celestial
rolling and turning

as the earth glides from darkness
back to darkness,
an unstoppable cycle
linking us
across the eons.

•

Against this unfolding dance,
the glow of firestones arose.

Solid black hills revealed
curving silhouettes moment
by moment.

•

> *Darkness holds*
> *a silent fertility*

•

Trees and nightbirds
resumed their murmurings, rustlings,
quiet calls,

wet earth exhaled its
freshly greened scent.

The empty bowl filled
with
mystery
upon mystery.

•

Behind me
I heard a voice say:

> *Today I held the eagle feather*
> *up to the sky.*
>
> *I showed it to the east,*
> *to the west,*

the north,
and the south.

The voice faded,
the firelight (a tiny star)
played, and

I gave thanks

for eagle feathers,
for sky,
and for the
empty
fertile
dark.

~~~~~

For Gene

Part V

Blessing

Forgive Me

Forgive me
if I seem
obsessed

with silences
and forests
and snowy limbs,

entranced by visions
of trees
overarching....

Forgive me if
grief and joy live side by side
in this altar, my heart....

Forgive me if I forget
that mistletoe
festoons itself over dying branches

(adorning death
with evergreenery
and white berries).

Forgive me if I yearn
with all my heart
for a snowy silence:

for midnight
in the forest—
and I don't know where the moon is....

•

Icy storms
whistle across field
and night;

yet every sparkling dawn,
silence reigns (and when snow wraps the trees,
they dance invisibly).

Here in the forest
(or the desert, sea, or city center),
rests the soul of the world—

here,
(unavoidable)
our insignificance—

here, our equality
with grub and fallen log;
bear; eagle; quivering leaf; frozen stream....

Here, silence invites
our grief and fear
(powerless, hairless, weaponless).

> *Welcome, Friend,*
> *to Infinity—*
>
> *to vastness unimaginable,*
> *to love unmatchable.*

This is the place
where God whispers!

And where I realize
the answer to all of my problems

is *thank you....*

~~~~~

Song of the White Dove

The white dove came again....

I love how she sits far back
in the black, tangled branches
of that wild oak tree.

(She glows through the falling darkness,
a phantom of herself.)

She used to frighten me,
appearing unannounced
at nightfall.

You're not from around here, are you,
I thought at her,
that first night.

•

I've tried to make up all kinds of stories
about why she visits when she does—

a harbinger of death?
Of change?

Well—every day changes and dies,
as do we....

•

Her song differs
from those of the mourning doves
that have surrounded me
since birth

(my father taught me their song.)

Softer than theirs,
it floats featherlike, unmournful;

it curls,

wispy,
tender,
wraithlike
(holy....)

•

We have watched each other
for years now,

through black ash
and smoky grey.

We stare together,
dual-captured,
at myriad blue-white
starfields

(our secret.)

•

Her song always
stops me midstep,
midbreath,
midquestion,
an inner
gasp.

An elder's words
come back to me,
and I realize
that she sings
not as a warning of death,

but with the
encouragement
to keep
dying....

~~~~~

(Recalling the wisdom
of Chungliang al Huang,
who appears in Finding Joe,
a film by Patrick Takaya Solomon.)

Stumbling

Lately I sense
something building
out in the ethers.

I see an extraordinary
jumbling of
improbable, gorgeous
clouds—

a net of diamonds
coalescing
in the night sky—

a knitting together
of unspoken hopes
and spoken dreams.

It's happening in the silence
that infuses acceptance,
gratitude, consideration....

It's happening in the
mistakes I make,

the clumsy words that
spill out,

in my deepest unknowing....

•

What is required of me now
is no more
(and no less)
than to continue
living
exactly
as
I
am:

devoted
(and sentenced)
to learning,
to the irredeemable pain
and joy (like a mist)
that crowd each
conscious moment,

to stumbling through
my truth—

and finding a way
to turn that stumbling
into
dance.

~~~~~

Reconciling Grey

Sometimes all the beauty
in the world

seems to vanish
in one whoosh.

Death bookends life,

fate turns on its dime,

and rugs shift
under our feet.

Poems, words, colors, disappear—
metaphor leaves....

Shall we hope for no more happiness,
if gifts come
on the sharp edge
of a knife?

•

Perhaps I have fought the grey too long—
perhaps grey needs to be my new favorite color.

Do I lose all color?
Do I merely note loss?

Do I thank God for
this opportunity to
find myself alone in the dark,

reaching out to something
more powerful than my own tiny humanity?

I don't know.

Everything I think I know
is really everything we can't ever understand.

•

This morning
I stood on my front steps—
and this foreign wind
played in my hair,

ran all around my face,
and made me dizzy.

Birds sang confusingly
of nests and mates
and territories....

The sun shone strangely
spring-like,

and I brought in the laundry,
fresh and crisp.

~~~~~

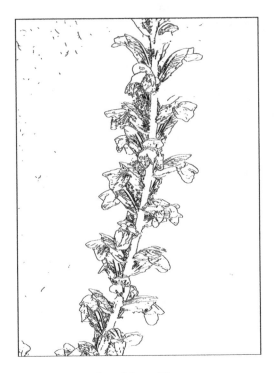

Our Next Fire

A gathering of guides and angels
meets to discuss our cases

when we're asleep,
exhausted from our efforts.

For lengthy stretches
they trail behind us,
sending only dustings of compassion
to drift over our saddened souls.

As we embark,
hesitating,
across the sea that
both buoys and threatens,

as we learn to catch
the breath of love
in our own sails,

steering our lives by it,
allowing it to penetrate
the veils over our hearts—

as we feel ourselves stirred
and wakened
by the great
energies,

the uncontrollable
motions
around
and under us—

as we give our lives over
to something we can't understand

and surrender, under grace, to its lead—

every time we brave
this chill, unpromising wind,

the angels take note,

and begin kindling
our next
fire....

~~~~~

The Youngest

Imagine living in a place
where everything you walk by
has a meaning,

where your history,
the history of your family,
the history of your ancestors
walks beside you....

> *On this corner*
> *an ancient great uncle died*
> *fighting Roman invaders—*
> *(or maybe he was the invader.)*

That tower holds the remains of
royal prisoners,
queens,
princes;

it holds jeweled swords and scabbards,
crowns, uniforms,
crosses, capes....

History lives in our bones.

That church spire across the river,
a place where you sometimes sit
to enjoy the silence,
has witnessed coronations,
baptisms,
executions....

Who were the builders?

This pub
(where we have haddock and a pint)
is the same one which heard a
famous writers' club plot and share
their mystic tales....

What if you lived in a place
where every grove and stone
held a family story?

*That copse of aspen
is where your great grandparents
got married;*

*that hollow stone in the ground,
where you played as a child,*

is where your grandma crushed
dried corn;

The bicycle in the garage
is the one your father learned on....

The land, the minerals
all around and in you
hold you together,
hold all the stories....

What if you never felt alone
or abandoned,

because you
are
just
the youngest....

~~~~~

[draft magic]

When times seem dark,
draft magic.

Oh, you can pedal really hard,
sweat and gasp for breath,
(and yes, oh yes, I do this)

> *Work, play, rest,*
> *work, cook, pay,*

listen, listen, listen,
respond, work,
      rest, pay.

Once in a while,
some huge object whizzes
past me, and whoosh!
I am boosted
by its wake.

While drafting,
you can sit up for a second,
breathe, and look around!

Running out the door one morning,
I paused on my front step, glanced up,
and noticed a complete rainbow,
left to right!

Wait! A double rainbow!
[magic!]

Catalina appearing again
through drifting smoke,

a cloudburst, a downpour
after drought—

when you can, remember to draft.

[Magic] *waits* for our attention.

Whew.
[*thanks!*]

~~~~~

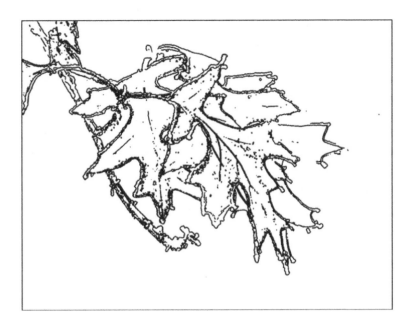

Mnemosyne

Nag.

Frankincense.

Myyrh.

Lavender, tea, coffee,
baking bread, roasting nuts,

cinnamon, corn,
freshly turned earth,

crushed garlic, basil leaves, sweet sage,

desert minerals,
mountain pines.

Memories ripple and rush,
a torrent, a gentle brush,
unbidden, undeniable,
unmanageable,
unwanted
perhaps.

Released by a faint whiff
of nag champa,
these visit:

> searches,
> vanished loves,
>
> crystals,
> candles,
>
> astrology charts,
> old friends,
>
> chants, churches
> ceremonies, landkeepers....

Following a curl of grey smoke
rising from a censor,

Love wells, remembering
a young person alone,
bitter, terrified.

I celebrate a new Way:
Revisioning rather than Seeking,
Tenderness in place of Despair,
Recognition, not Fear.

I love, now, my own magic
and my own trepidation.

I love that all Surface Crazy
reflects an Underworld of Grace.

We are connected to everything in this world
through millions of yards of neurons....

Scents arrive,
olfactory cells send signals
to your brain, your body:

we are
electrified matter,
mater.

How shall we attune to what's on offer?

Horrifying *and* sacred:

the whole wide universe
sparkles and simmers.

~~~~~

Thanks to Divine Harmony for the above question.
https://divineharmony.com/

The Black Sun

So many starry nights lately
in this usually fog-kissed land!

Sitting between fire and prayer,
I watch the play:

A beginner crescent moon
lilts through the sky-arc.

Stars bow out of her way
as she passes.

I watch swirls of bats dart and trill,
feeding among the buggy clouds.

On nights like this one,
the sky bodies seem to dance for the earth

(except Venus,
standing resolute and steady,
beaming her silver-gold defiance.)

I am transfixed by the starshow,
Venus, and the moon.

Atmospheric water
changes the light into pastels
so deep and clear
I feel I could fall right up into them....

The Black Sun
glows
after all hope
of warmth is lost.

Its promise appears
in fountains of sparks
floating into the sky
after one has accepted
the death of light.

Its fire comforts in our darkest dark.

I sit as living proof
of the survival of dreams.
I live in the company of the Mystery.

Guided by its shifting Light,
I know myself as one spark
dancing among all of these lights,
great and small.

~~~~~

Among the Gratitudes

Silence.
Holy.

Out in the yard,
under a crystal sailing moon,

under the silent
blast of starlight eons old,

black branches etch
the night

and call down the silence....

•

I stand amazed again,
surprised
by this
ever available presence
that waits,

always patiently,

for my notice....

•

Perhaps
holding a spot
for Silence within

serves the greater good....

Amid the cacophony
of modern life,

the chatter
of thoughts;

amid the ten thousand
worries,

among the gratitudes;

a space of silence.

Evocative
Reverent
Receptive
Reflective

Oh my heart,
my heart—

How do I hold all I love
inside you?

How do I wrap you
all about

with this
most precious
Silence?

~~~~~

About the Author

Beth Anne Boardman, RN, MA, PhD lives in California and New Hampshire. She travels and lectures on the Mythology of Sport; Women and Myth; and the Alchemy of Adolescence, in addition to consulting as a writer to websites. Her career spans work as a registered nurse, grant-writer, the study of world dance and music, and the profound joy of raising two children. She received her PhD in Mythology with an emphasis in Depth Psychology for the successful defense of her dissertation, *Diving into Darkness: Adolescents in the United States,* available on ProQuest.

Cover Art: "Mexican Blanket"

Gail Broadbent Firmin's watercolors reflect her love of nature. Inspired by the beauty of the valley where she lives, scenes from her travels, or just the lazy repose of her two cats, she strives for a semblance of realism, while having fun with the properties of different pigments and techniques. Primarily self-taught, she has enjoyed the opportunity to participate in workshops with artists such as Frank Francese and Michael Atkinson and continues her education in the arts by taking classes and workshops with local instructors. Gail has volunteered since 2006 as an art therapist for disabled adults with the DDRC (Developmental Disability Resource Center) and teaches art classes for the City of Lakewood's adult continuing education programs. She is the social media and PR manager for the Lakewood Arts Council and a member of their Co-op Gallery. More of her work can be seen at: <u>Acornucopia</u>.

Made in the USA
Monee, IL
05 October 2020

44002896R00075